This book

If found, please contact me at:

mithmoth

Made in the USA
Las Vegas, NV
23 May 2025

22599579R00073